Twelve modern designs inspired by

CAPITOL KNITS

America's capital, Washington DC

by Tanis Gray
AUTHOR OF *KNIT LOCAL*

TO CALLUM
MY LITTLE PATRIOT

Copyright © 2012 Tanis Gray

Flag (this page) copyright © Jnn13
(Creative Commons Attribution-Share Alike 3.0 Unported license)
Protesters (page 7) and cherry blossoms (page 53)
copyright © Jake Landis
All other photographs copyright © Tanis Gray
Illustrations copyright © Paul Heaston

All rights reserved.
These patterns are for personal use only.
Reproduction, distribution and sale
of these patterns in any form is prohibited.

ISBN 978-1467990219

Printed in the United States of America

Graphic design by Mary Joy Gumayagay

TABLE OF CONTENTS

4–5	Table of Contents
6–7	Introduction
8–23	**Sweaters**
10–11	Landmarks
24–51	**Accessories**
26–27	Landmarks
52–53	**Abbreviations**
53	Pattern Skill Levels
53	Conversions
54–55	**Resources**
56	Acknowledgments

12 AMERICAN INDIAN CARDIGAN

American Indian Museum
White Ash (*Fraxinus americana*)

14 JEFFERSON PULLOVER

Jefferson Memorial
Black Walnut (*Juglans nigra*)

34 LIBRARY OF CONGRESS HAT

Court of Neptune Fountain
Yellow Buckeye (*Aesculus flava*)

36 SUMMERHOUSE HAT & WRISTERS

Summerhouse
Osage Orange
(*Maclura pomifera*)

40 RENWICK WRISTERS

Renwick Gallery
Sugar Maple (*Acer saccharum*)

Washington, DC has a surprising amount of urban forest. With well over 100,000 trees alone, including the world-famous cherry blossoms that bloom in springtime, trees improve the air quality, provide shade, aid in protecting the water supply and save energy. Trees native to the DC area include the White Ash, Black Walnut, Burr Oak, Northern Red Oak, Elm, Yellow Buckeye, Osage Orange, Sugar Maple, Swamp Maple Oak, Tulip and the White Oak, to name a few. The leaves of these trees are represented by the leaf motif behind each page number.

The Red Maple (Acer Rubrum) thrives all over eastern North America, reaching maturity at 70 to 80 years. Its leaves grace all the non-pattern pages in this book.

20 LINCOLN CARDIGAN

Lincoln Memorial
Burr Oak (*Quercus macrocarpa*)

28 UNION STATION INFINITY COWL

Union Station
Northern Red Oak
(*Quercus rubra*)

32 E PLURIBUS UNUM COWL

The White House
American Elm
(*Ulmus americana*)

42 CONSTITUTION HALL SCARF

Daughters of the American Revolution Constitution Hall
Swamp White Oak
(*Quercus bicolor*)

46 CAPITOL SHAWL

Capitol Building
American Tulip
(*Liriodendron tulipifera*)

48 NATIONAL GALLERY SHAWL

National Gallery of Art
White Oak (*Quercus alba*)

A LOVE LETTER TO WASHINGTON DC

I adore Washington DC. There is an incredible amount of history and culture in a space smaller than 70 square miles. Marble, columns, statues, engravings, books, artifacts, monuments, museums, markets, and gardens, this city has it in spades and all were the inspiration for this collection of knitwear.

This is my love letter to this great city. Instead of pen and paper, I used fiber and color to express my admiration and share the allure and charm of this town with other knitters. The locations in *Capitol Knits* are ones I walk to often with my son in his stroller and stare in wonder at what others have created. I feel fortunate to have these

From left to right: Giant stone urns flank the steps on the backside of the Supreme Court building where the words "Justice for Liberty" are inscribed. ★ Both sides of the Capitol Building are considered the "front" but the East front side is the only way to enter the complex nowadays. ★ Protesters exercise their first amendment right against the war in Iraq on the National Mall. ★ The Ulysses S. Grant memorial located at the base of Capitol Hill faces the direction of the

locations in my backyard and even luckier that they inspire my work as much as they do. I've lived in many cities since leaving home many years ago and never felt as at home in any of them as I do in DC.

A MEMBER OF THE DAUGHTERS OF THE AMERICAN REVOLUTION, I am proud to call such a culturally rich area home. Each block of this monumental city carries with it a long and important history as strong and diverse as our young country. I feel more patriotic here, more inspired to get up and fight for something I believe in and continually appreciative of what others who have come before me have done to make this country a better place.

I HOPE YOU ENJOY THIS COLLECTION and that it inspires you as much as this marvelous town inspires me each day.

From sea to shining sea,

Tanis

Lincoln Memorial and is the second largest equestrian sculpture in the United States. ★ This way to the Capitol where millions visit each year! ★ The unofficial entrance to Chinatown, the Friendship Archway has seven roofs reaching up to 60 feet, 7000 tiles and 272 painted dragons. It is the largest single-span archway in the world.

GANAMERICANINDIANCARDIGANJEFFERSONPULLOVERLINCOLNCARDIGANAMERICANIN

ARDIGANJEFFERSONPULLOVERLINCOLNCARDIGAN**SWEATERS**AMERICANINDIANCARDI

SWEATERS

Looking for inspiration? Keep your eyes open. Inspiration is everywhere, whether it's the architecture, on a wall in a museum, the clothes on your back or a random memory. The key is to keep your eyes and mind open at all times. We live in a world so bursting with sensory overload that it can be difficult to filter your senses.

The following sweater designs are based on three of my favorite locations in the city, the American Indian Museum, the Jefferson Memorial and the Lincoln Memorial. While it's fun to visit during the height of tourist season and watch people see the grandeur for the first time, I prefer visiting when it's quiet to observe them in peace.

The American Indian Cardigan was designed to mimic the texture on the outside of this unique building as well as the intricate beadwork many

of the tribes excel at. The warm color of the yarn brings forth memories of a college semester spent in New Mexico exploring the art and spirituality of the southwest, where many of my teachers were members of American Indian tribes. They taught me a different way to appreciate nature and beauty and I reminisce often on my time spent there.

THE JEFFERSON MEMORIAL IS UNUSUAL IN THAT IT IS OPEN ON ALL SIDES to the elements. While the inside is a visual delight of engraved walls, a textured ceiling, a statue and carved marble, I find the exterior of the building to be even lovelier. Large, intimidating columns were the inspiration for the back and sleeves of the pullover that are covered in twisting cables. A simple reverse stockinette front brings to mind the elegant smoothness of the marble floor, while the blue evokes the waters of the Tidal Basin found directly out front.

THE LINCOLN MEMORIAL IS A FAVORITE OF MANY. Nestled in direct line with the Reflecting Pool, the World War II Memorial and the Washington Monument, the thoughtful geometry of its location inspired simple cables. One of my favorite Lincoln quotes reads, "All my life I have tried to pluck a thistle and plant a flower wherever the flower would grow in thought and mind" which is mimicked in the thistle design climbing up the back of the cardigan. The color of the yarn reflects the color of the milk thistle.

From left to right: Sunrise at the Lincoln Memorial, designed in the style of a Greek temple with 36 large columns. ★ The Jefferson Memorial at a distance rests peacefully on the banks of the Tidal Basin. ★ Thomas Jefferson greets visitors inside the main entrance of his memorial. ★ The graceful swoop of the American Indian Museum's exterior makes this building unlike any other in the city.

AMERICAN INDIAN CARDIGAN

Approximate finished size 34 (38, 42, 46, 50)" bust, buttoned

Materials 5 (5, 6, 6, 7) hanks Blue Sky Alpacas *Worsted Hand Dyes* (3½ oz / 100g; approx 100 yds / 91m; 50% Royal Alpaca, 50% Merino) in #2010 Rusty Orange (A) and 1 hank #2003 Ecru (B) ✕ US9 knitting needles and dpns ✕ 4 stitch markers, tapestry needle, J / 10 crochet hook, 3 1¼" buttons

Gauge 13 sts and 26 rows over 4" in seed st

Part of the Smithsonian and opening in 2004, the NATIONAL MUSEUM OF THE AMERICAN INDIAN *is the largest museum in the country dedicated to preserving the art, language, history and the lifestyle of the American Indians of the west. The unique curvilinear building designed by Douglas Cardinal and John Paul Jones is covered in amber-colored Kasota limestone designed to mimic natural rock formations shaped by wind and water over thousands of years and is surrounded by "wetlands" on the exterior. It is home to more than 800,000 objects and 125,000 images, many from the Heye Foundation.*

The WHITE ASH *(Fraxinus americana) is one of the most in-demand trees for making household objects. With dense, strong-grained white wood, it is used for baseball bats, tool handles, electric guitars and lobster traps.*

Body

With A, CO 60 (60, 60, 68, 68) sts, do not join into round, pm after 10 (10, 10, 12, 12) sts for front, 10 sts for sleeve, 20 (20, 20, 24, 24) sts for back, 10 sts for sleeve, 10 (10, 10, 12, 12) sts for front.

Work *k1, p1* seed st for 2 rows.

Next row (RS): *Work in seed st to 1 st before marker, m1, k1, slm, k1, m1,* repeat to end of row—8 sts inc.
Next row (WS): Work across row in seed st, working raglan sleeve seams in stockinette st.

Continue until there are 56 (62, 68, 74, 82) sts between markers for back, 28 (31, 34, 37, 41) for each fronts and 46 (52, 58, 60, 68) sts between each sleeve—204 (228, 252, 268, 300) sts.

AT THE SAME TIME, work buttonholes. When work measures 1½" from CO edge on RS, work 3 sts in seed st, BO 3, work to end of row. On WS, work across row in seed st to gap, CO 3 sts, work to end of row. Work 2nd buttonhole 2½" from 1st, repeat for 3rd buttonhole.

Next row: Work across row in pattern, placing sleeve sts on scrap yarn, CO 3 sts at each underarm—118 (130, 142, 154, 170) sts.

Continue in pattern until work measures 7 (7½, 8, 8½, 9)" from underarm.

BO in seed st.

Sleeves

Transfer sts from scrap yarn to dpns, CO 3 sts at underarm and pm for beginning of round—49 (55, 61, 63, 71) sts.

Next round: *K2tog, k1* to end of round, end k1 (1, 1, 0, 2)—33 (37, 41, 42, 48) sts.

BO in seed st.

Repeat for other sleeve.

Finishing

With crochet hook and B, work single crochet around all edges.

Weave in all loose ends with tapestry needle.

Block.

Sew on buttons to correspond with buttonholes.

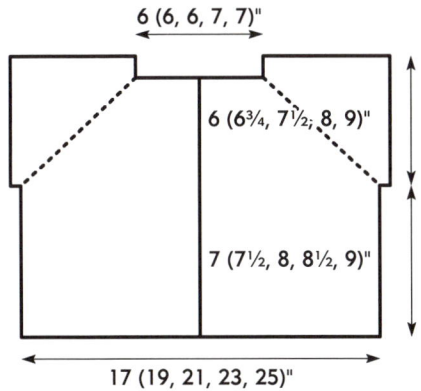

JEFFERSON PULLOVER

Approximate finished size 34 (38, 42, 46, 50)" bust

Materials 5 (6, 6, 7, 8) hanks Imperial Yarn *Native Twist* (4 oz / 113g; approx 150 yds / 137m; 100% Wool) in #101 Teal Heather ✕ US10 circular knitting needle and dpns, US8 circular knitting needle and dpns ✕ 4 stitch markers, tapestry needle, cable needle

Gauge 11 sts and 17 rows over 4" in reverse stockinette st in the round using US10 needle

Body

With US8 needle, CO 44 (44, 48, 52, 56) sts, join into round, being careful not to twist sts, pm for beginning of round.

Work *k2, p2* rib until work measures 1¼" from CO edge.

Switch to US10 needle.

Next round: P6 across sleeve, pm, p16 (16, 18, 20, 22) across back, pm, p6 across sleeve, pm, p16 (16, 18, 20, 22) across front.

On every other round, inc 1 st on each side of each marker—8 sts inc.

AT THE SAME TIME, work cable chart on back of sweater and down sleeves.

NOTE: Center pattern on sleeves and back. On back, note that chart is 66 sts wide. Begin by working the center 16 (16, 18, 20, 22) sts from chart, and add sts from chart on each side as work increases until all chart sts are worked, noting that the full width of the chart will only be worked on the 2 largest sizes. Work remaining sts in reverse stockinette st.

Continue until there are 44 (50, 56, 60, 66) sts between markers for back and front and 34 (40, 44, 46, 50) sts between each sleeve—156 (180, 200, 212, 232) sts.

Next round: Work across row in pattern, placing sleeve sts on scrap yarn, CO 3 sts at each underarm—94 (106, 118, 126, 138) body sts.

Continue in pattern until work measures 14 (14½, 15, 15½, 16)" from underarm.

Switch to US8 needle, work *k2, p2* ribbing for 10 rows.

BO in rib.

In honor of our third president, the Jefferson Memorial *was built in 1943 and designed by John Russell Pope. Due to a bronze shortage because of WWII, a plaster version of the 25 foot interior sculpture painted to look like bronze was installed temporarily. The finished bronze sculpture of Jefferson was added in the center four years later in 1947. Surrounded by circular marble steps, a portico, Ionic columns, and a shallow dome, the building has open sides and is exposed to the elements. Excerpts from Jefferson's writing adore the walls.*

A member of the hickory family, the Black Walnut *(Juglans nigra) is more resistant to frost than other trees and reaches great heights. Often used for flooring, furniture and rifle stocks, its nuts are pressed for oil and used in cooking.*

Sleeves

Transfer 34 (40, 44, 46, 50) sleeve sts from waste yarn to US10 dpns, CO 3 sts at underarm and pm for beginning of round—37 (43, 47, 49, 53) sts.

While continuing in cable pattern down sleeve, dec on each side of marker (p2tog) every round until 31 sts remain.

Work even for 2½".

Next round: Dec on each side of marker—29 sts.

Work until sleeve measures 8½" from underarm.

Switch to US8 dpns.

Next round: K2tog, *p2, k2* to last 3 sts, end p2, k1—28 sts.

On opposite sleeve, work k1, *p2, k2* to last 4 sts, end p2, k2tog.

Work *k2, p2* ribbing for 10 rounds.

BO in rib.

Repeat for other sleeve.

Finishing

Weave in all loose ends with tapestry needle.

Block.

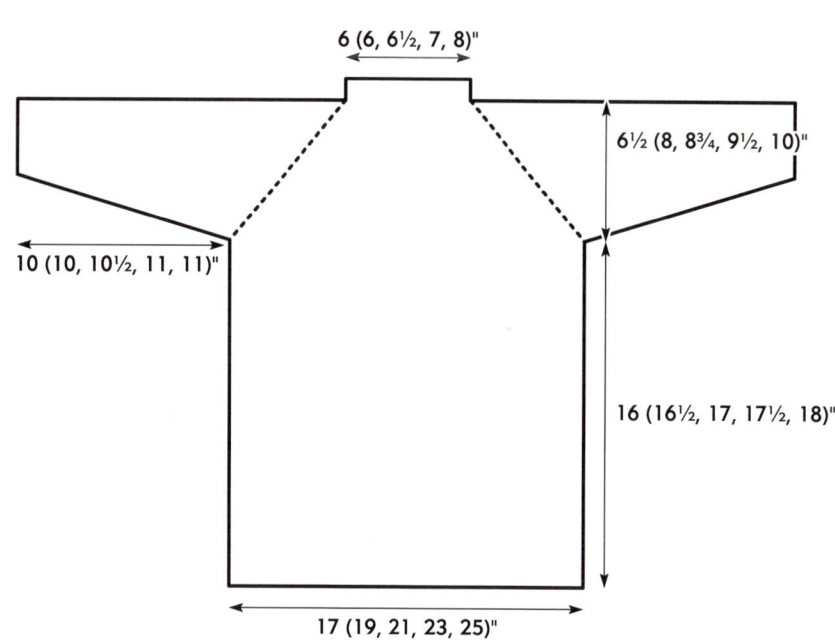

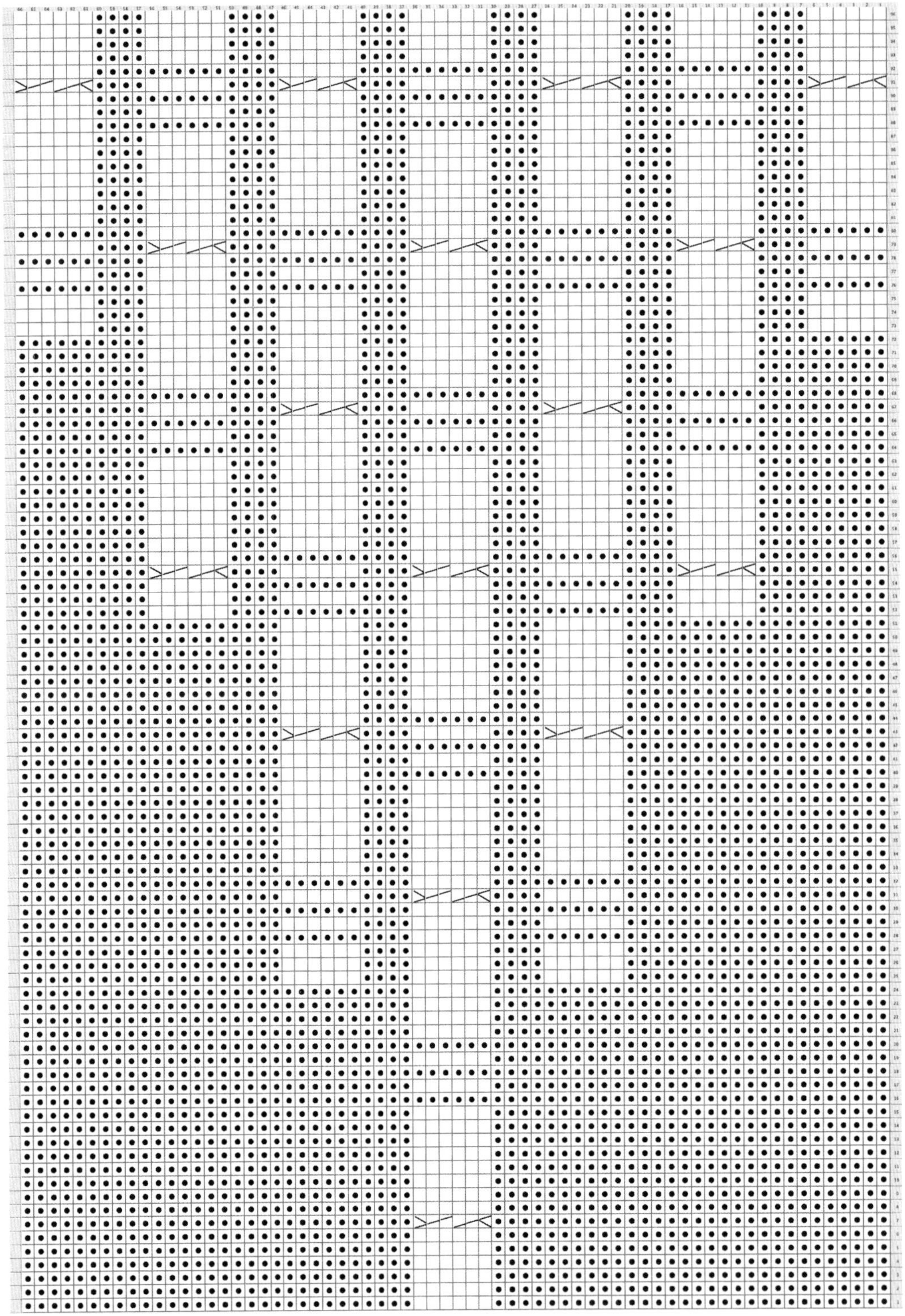

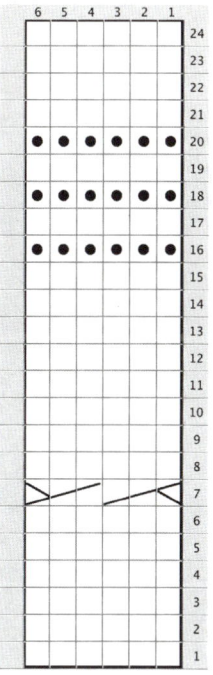

☐ knit

● purl

⤬⤬⤬ **c3 over 3 right**
Sl 3 sts to cn and hold to back, k3, k3 from cn.

LINCOLN CARDIGAN

Erected on the National Mall in 1922 and designed by Henry Bacon, the LINCOLN MEMORIAL *honors our 16th President. The exterior of the monument mimics a Greek temple finished in yule marble and contains a 19-foot, 159-ton seated sculpture of Lincoln by Daniel Chester French. Inscriptions of the* Gettysburg Address *and his* Second Inaugural Address *are chiseled on the walls, and Martin Luther King's* I Have A Dream *speech was given there in 1963. The memorial can be seen on the back of the penny and $5 bill with Lincoln's face adorning the front.*

A deciduous, fire-resistant tree, the BURR OAK *(Quercus macrocarpa) grows tall and wide with a trunk sometimes as thick as 3' wide. A slow grower, they can live up to 400 years and have the largest acorns of all the oaks.*

Approximate finished size 34 (38, 42, 46, 50)" bust, buttoned

Materials 4 (5, 5, 6, 6) hanks Red Barn Yarn *Plied Worsted* (4 oz / 113g; approx 250 yds / 229m; 100% Wool) in Coral Bells ✕ US8 circular knitting needle and dpns, US6 circular knitting needle ✕ 4 stitch markers, tapestry needle, G / 6 crochet hook, waste yarn, 7 ¾" buttons

Gauge 16 sts and 24 rows over 4" in stockinette st using US8 needle

Body

With US8 needle, provisionally CO 65 (69, 77, 81, 85) sts, do not join into round, pm after 14 (15, 17, 18, 19) sts for front, 8 sts for sleeve, 21 (23, 27, 29, 31) sts for back, 8 sts for sleeve, 14 (15, 17, 18, 19) sts for front.

First and last 5 sts are worked in garter st to form button band throughout sweater.

Make buttonholes every 3½" by k2, yo, k2tog, k1 on button band.

On every other round, inc 1 st by working a yo on each side of each marker—8 sts inc.

AT THE SAME TIME, work cable chart on back of sweater and cable chart down sleeves and fronts.

NOTE: Center pattern on sleeves and back. On back, note that chart is 35 sts wide. Begin by working the center 21 (23, 27, 29, 31) sts from chart, and add sts from chart on each side as work increases until all chart sts are worked. On fronts, work chart next to button band on each side. Work remaining sts in stockinette st.

Continue until there are 67 (75, 83, 91, 99) sts between markers for back, 37 (41, 45, 49, 53) sts on each front and 54 (60, 64, 70, 76) sts between each sleeve—249 (277, 301, 329, 357) sts.

Next row: Work across row in pattern, placing sleeve sts on waste yarn—141 (157, 173, 189, 205) body sts.

Continue in pattern until work measures 15 (15½, 16, 16½, 17)" from underarm.

Switch to US6 needle, work garter st for 8 rows.

BO in knit.

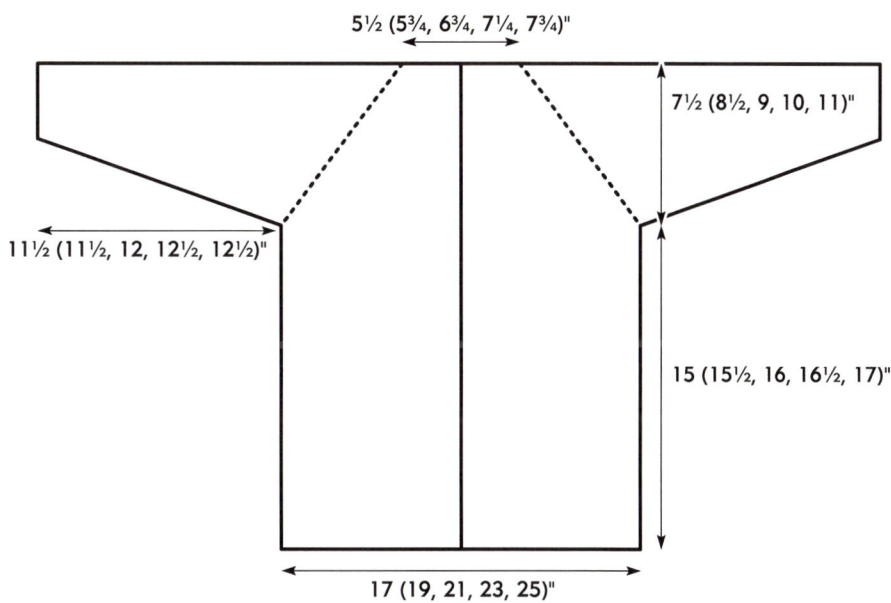

Sleeves

Place 54 (60, 64, 70, 76) sleeve sts on US8 dpns, pm at underarm.

Continuing cable pattern, dec 1 st on each side of marker (2 sts dec) every 4th round until 36 (36, 40, 40, 44) sts remain, then work even until sleeve measures 10 (10, 10½, 11, 11)".

Work 2 rounds in pattern.

Work 10 rounds of garter (knit 1 row, purl 1 row in the round).

BO in knit.

Repeat for other sleeve.

Finishing

Pull out waste yarn at neck edge and with US8 needle, work garter st for 4".

BO in knit.

Weave in all loose ends with tapestry needle.

Block lightly.

Sew on buttons to correspond with buttonholes.

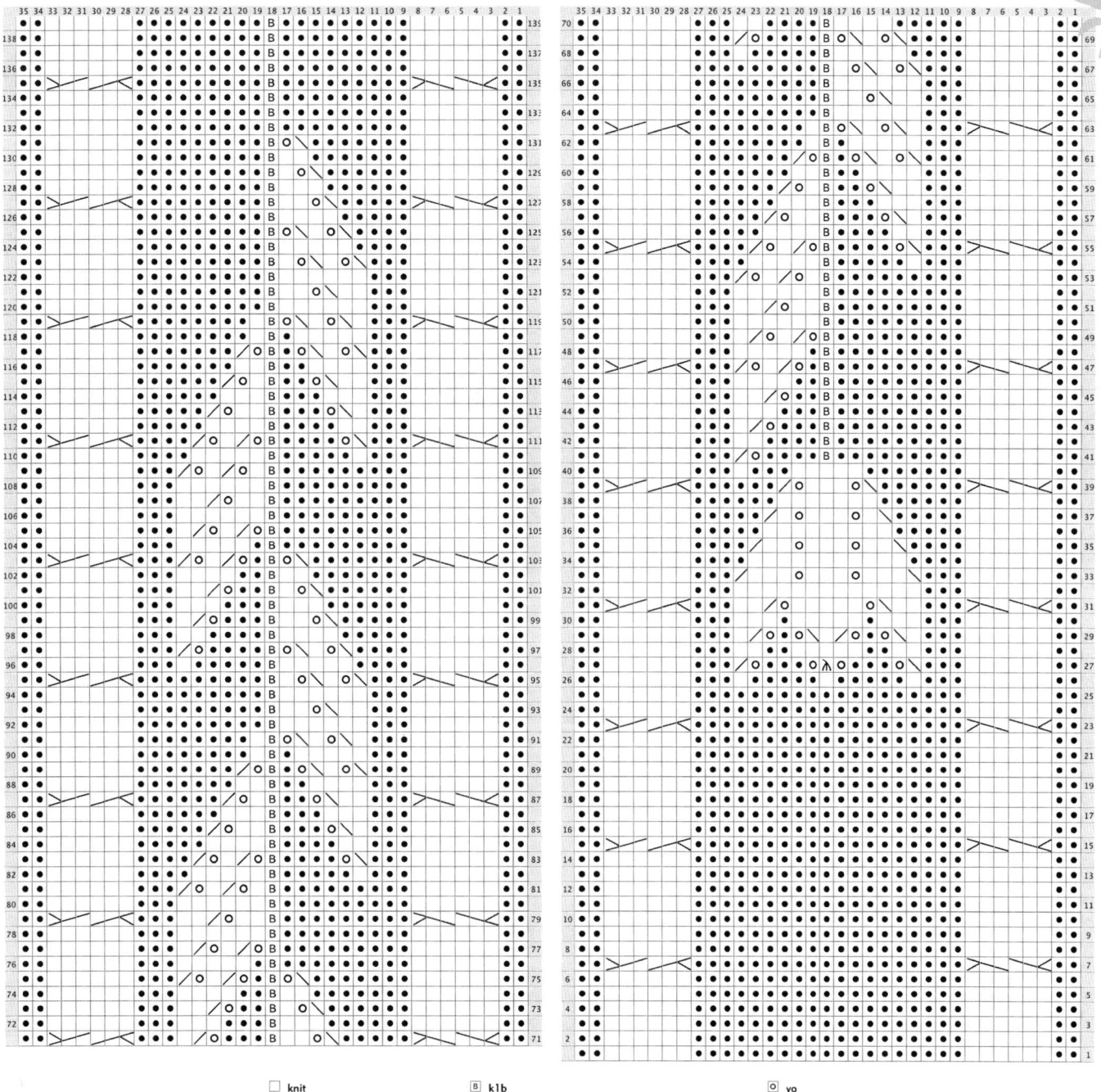

	knit		k1b		yo
	RS: knit stitch		RS: knit through back loop of st		
	WS: purl stitch		WS: purl		sk2p
	purl		c3 over 3 left		k2tog
	RS: purl stitch		Sl 3 sts to cn, hold in front, k3, k3 from cn.		
	WS: knit stitch		c3 over 3 right		ssk
			Sl 3 sts to cn, hold in back, k3, k3 from cn.		

FINITYCOWLEPLURIBUSUNUMCOWLLIBRARYOFCONGRESSHATSUMMERHOUSEHAT&WRI

RENWICKWRISTERSCONSTITUTIONHALLSCARF**ACCESSORIES**CAPITOLSHAWLNATION

ACCESSORIES

There are so many amazing places in cities. Tiny little nooks you happen upon accidentally, hidden gems you find when you get lost, locations in long forgotten areas and places so new they haven't even made it into the latest guide books. I liken these discoveries to the joy you experience when you come across a missing treasure, or a $20 bill found in the pocket of last winter's coat.

I walk through Union Station almost every day. You can be trapped in a crowd of people so thick you move as one giant unit, or stroll through during off-peak hours when it's so quiet you can hear your footsteps echo across the marble floor, I love this train station. With hustle and bustle being the watchwords of any major transportation hub, the business of the Fair Isle infinity cowl captures the essence of people running every which way, all different colors, sizes and shapes.

E Pluribus Unum is the Latin motto of the United States and translates to "out of many, one." The White House is one of the many beating hearts in Washington DC, whether the President is kicking back and watching a football game with his family or working hard to make our country better with his staff. The multiple picot hems of the lace cowl remind us of the many issues the White House is working on at any given time.

From left to right: The Great Hall inside the Library of Congress has embellished ceilings covered with paintings and sculptures by over 50 American painters and sculptors. ★ The West exterior of the Library of Congress is home to the Court of Neptune Fountain, where Neptune reigns supreme surrounded by water nymphs and sea creatures. ★ Often thought of as the rear entrance, The North Lawn of the White House is actually the front and official entrance. ★ Located next to the West Wing of the White House, the Eisenhower Executive Office Building houses much of the White House staff. ★ The Grand Salon of

The Library of Congress has arguably the most beautiful interior space in all of Washington DC. Covered in ornate paintings, sculpture, textured ceilings, and books, it is the exterior that often goes unnoticed. In the front of the building tucked away so it often is missed is the Court of Neptune Fountain. Here Neptune reigns with his court surrounded by light posts with purple globes. The churning of the water and robustness of the sculpture inspired an unusual cabled and lace hat.

The Summerhouse is my absolute favorite location in the entire city. A true hidden gem, it is often walked by completely unnoticed. A small structure made of stone and brick covered in bright green moss, the iron latticework brought to mind cabled and lattice-like lace. It was this location that inspired *Capitol Knits*.

The Renwick Gallery sits across the street from the White House. Housing some incredible works of art, many people hustle by, unaware of the treasures it holds. At the top of the red velvet covered staircase is a large yellow hall with dark railings. A sparkly chandelier watches over each visitor and inspired striped, slightly sparkly wristers.

A new member of the Daughters of the American Revolution, I spent many an afternoon at the DAR Library and Constitution Hall doing research on my family tree. The enormous building takes up an entire city block and has many little nooks and crannies around its façade. The American flag hangs proudly out front and the scarf is meant to reflect its stripes with the lace edging a nod to the giant support columns it hangs between.

The Capitol is truly a sight to behold. What struck me the first time I saw it was its sheer size. An old world feel in a modern city, the enormous building itself is surrounded by extensive lawns peppered with flora and fauna. The marble steps, green grass, outlying buildings and geometry of the grounds inspired a simple shawl. Topped with "mini domes" around the edge, this is the perfect shawl for a stroll around the Capitol.

The two large buildings that make up the National Gallery of Art couldn't be more different. One sleek and modern, the other ornate and traditional, they are connected underground by an LED tunnel. Another one of my favorite hidden gems, it's not uncommon for me to walk back and forth through the tunnel a few times in a row. Combining modern and traditional design in one garment, the 2 versions of the shawl are the same except for the colors. Much like the 2 wings of the museum, the modern blue and silver version has brass rings in the yarn that shimmer in the sun just like the LED tunnel, while the dark pink version has a more traditional, romantic feel.

the Renwick Gallery with its distinct rose-colored walls is over 4,300 square feet and has ceilings that reach 40 feet. With works of art hung salon style, this gallery is often the setting for concerts and talks hosted by the Smithsonian. ★ A 200 foot underground passageway between the old and new wings of the National Gallery is an inter-active work of art made of LEDs called *Multiverse* by Leo Villareal. ★ Situated in Capitol Hill, Eastern Market is the oldest continually operated fresh food public market. Home to an incredible selection of meat, cheese, food, flowers, crafts and fine art, this is a local treasure.

UNION STATION INFINITY COWL

Approximate finished size 4½" wide by 63" circumference

Materials Brooklyn Tweed *Shelter* (1¾ oz / 50g; 140 yds / 128m; 100% American Wool): 1 hank each in Pumpernickel (A, brown), Fossil (B, white), Sap (C, yellow), Almanac (D, dark blue), and Faded Quilt (E, light blue) ✕ US8 16" circular knitting needle and spare US8 knitting needle ✕ Waste yarn, stitch marker, G / 6 crochet hook, tapestry needle

Gauge 24 sts and 17 rows over 4" in Fair Isle pattern

Built in the Beaux-Arts and Neoclassical style, opening in 1907 and designed by Daniel H. Burnham, Union Station's arches symbolize a gateway or triumphal arch. The original tracks ran through the National Mall and were moved later as part of the "City Beautiful" movement. Reopening in 1988, after seven years of heavy restoration, more than 90,000 visitors pass through daily. Housing Amtrak, the Metro and a number of other modes of transportation, as well as retail and restaurants, Union Station is constructed primarily of marble, gold leaf, white granite and mahogany.

Reaching great heights and recognizable by its shiny bark, the Northern Red Oak (Quercus rubra) is adaptable to most soil types. A very porous wood, it is commonly used for flooring, veneer, interior trim and furniture.

Notes
Because the cowl is worked in a tube, there is no need to weave in ends, just make sure loose ends are secured on WS so unraveling does not occur.

Cast On
With waste yarn and crochet hook, provisionally CO 56 sts.

Join into round (cowl will be a tube), being careful not to twist sts, pm for beginning of round and begin working chart twice across each row.

Work rows 1–134 of chart twice, do not BO.

Finishing
Divide sts in half and 3 needle join with spare needle.

Remove waste yarn from beginning edge repeat as above.

Kitchener st ends together with tapestry needle.

Block well.

all stitches are knit

- ■ A (Pumpernickel)
- ☐ B (Fossil)
- ■ C (Sap)
- ■ D (Almanac)
- ■ E (Faded Quilt)

E PLURIBUS UNUM COWL

Home to the President and his family, THE WHITE HOUSE was originally built in 1800 and designed by James Hoban. The complex includes the Executive Residence, West Wing, Cabinet Room, Roosevelt Room, East Wing, and the Eisenhower Executive Office Building, which houses the executive offices of the President and Vice President. In 1814, the interior and almost all of the exterior were burnt to the ground by the British Army. Modeled after an English country home, it includes six stories, 55,000 feet of floor space, 132 rooms, 35 bathrooms, 412 doors, 147 windows, 28 fireplaces, eight staircases, three elevators, five full-time chefs, a tennis court, a bowling alley, a movie theater, a jogging track, a swimming pool, a putting green, a vegetable garden and a playground.

Instrumental to landscape architecture in the 19th and 20th centuries, the AMERICAN ELM (Ulmus americana) has recently been devastated by Dutch Elm Disease. Very pliable with interlocking grain, the wood is often used for wagon wheel hubs, chair seats and coffins.

Approximate finished size 9" deep by 24" circumference

Materials 2 hanks Artyarns *Ultramerino 8* (3½ oz / 100g; 188 yds / 172m; 100% Luxury Merino Wool) in #234 Greenish Blue ✕ 2 US8 16" circular knitting needles and spare US8 knitting needle ✕ Waste yarn, stitch marker, tapestry needle

Gauge 16½ sts and 22 rows over 4" in stockinette st

Stitch Guide
Lace Pattern
Round 1: P17.
Round 2: P17.
Round 3: [K1, yo, k6, k2tog, k2togb, k6, yo] six times across row.
Round 4: [K7, k2tog, k2togb, k6] six times across row.
Round 5: [K1, yo, k1, yo, k4, k2tog, k2togb, k4, yo, k1, yo] six times across row.
Round 6: [K7, k2tog, k2togb, k6] six times across row.
Round 7: [K1, yo, k1, yo, k1, yo, k1, yo, k2, k2tog, k2togb, k2, yo, k1, yo, k1, yo, k1,yo] six times across row.
Round 8: [K9, k2tog, k2togb, k8] six times across row.
Round 9: [K8, k2tog, k2togb, k7] six times across row.
Rounds 10, 11, 24, 25: P17.
Rounds 12, 13, 14, 15, 16, 18, 19, 20, 21, 22, 23: K17.
Round 17: [Yo, k2tog] across row.

Cast On
CO 102 sts, join into round, being careful not to twist sts, pm for beginning of round.

Work rounds 1–11 of chart.

On round 12, weave waste yarn through sts with tapestry needle to mark this round, continue with pattern and work through round 22.

Before working round 23, using spare needle, insert needle through all sts of marked round and remove waste yarn.

Round 23: Hold spare needle behind working needle as for 3 needle BO (folding the fabric to create a picot hem) and knit 1 st from front needle together with 1 st from back needle around.

Work to end of chart.

Repeat rounds 3–25 a total of four times.

BO loosely knitwise.

Finishing

Weave in all loose ends with tapestry needle.

Block.

- • purl
- ▓ no stitch
  placeholder—no stitch made
- ☐ knit
- ○ yo
- ╱ k2tog
- ╲ k2togb
  knit 2 stitches together through the back loops
- ⌇ joining row
  With spare needle, weave through sts on scrap yarn and pull up. 3-needle join together with sts on main needle.

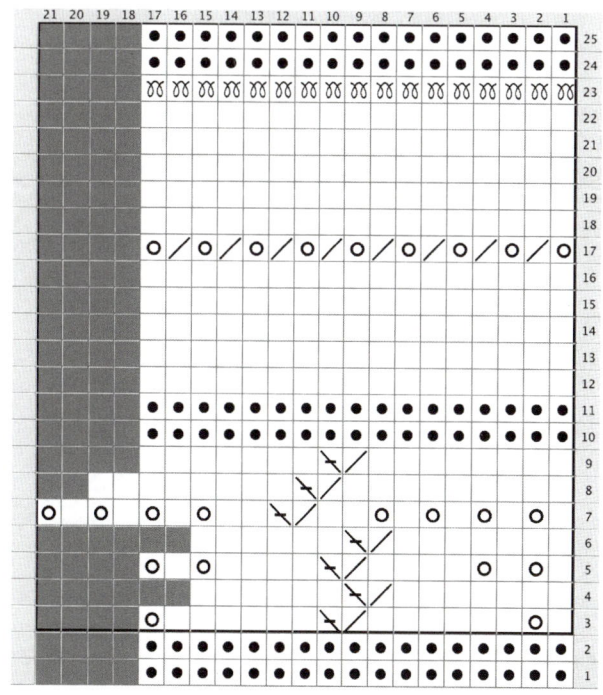

LIBRARY OF CONGRESS HAT

The oldest federal cultural institution in the United States, the original LIBRARY OF CONGRESS was burnt to the ground by invading British troops. Filled with what was considered one of the best personal collections at the time, Thomas Jefferson offered up his own collection of books and the newest library was built in 1886 after multiple incarnations elsewhere. Resting adjacent to the Capitol building, it was designed in the Italian Renaissance style by architects John L. Smithmeyer and Paul J. Pelz. It houses over 530 miles of shelves and over 140 million books.

A medium-sized deciduous tree, the YELLOW BUCKEYE (Aesculus flava) produces small, poisonous fruit. Used mainly for ornamentation, it blooms with yellow flowers in the spring.

Approximate finished size One size fits most adults, 22" circumference

Materials 1 hank Madelinetosh *Tosh Chunky* (3½ oz / 100g; 165 yds / 151m; 100% Superwash Merino Wool) in Sugar Plum ✕ US9 16" circular knitting needle and dpns ✕ Stitch marker, cable needle, tapestry needle

Gauge 15 sts and 19 rows over 4" in Lace & Cable Pattern

Stitch Guide
Lace & Cable Pattern
Rounds 1, 3, 5, 7, 9, 11: ([Yo, k2tog] four times, k8) five times.
Rounds 2, 4, 8, 10, 13, 15, 19, 21: Knit.
Round 6: (K8, c4 over 4 right) five times.
Rounds 12, 14, 16, 18, 20, 22: (K8, [yo, k2tog] four times) five times.
Round 17: (C4 over 4 left, k8) five times.

Repeat rounds 1–22 for pattern

Cast On
CO 74 sts, join into round, being careful not to twist sts, pm for beginning of round.

Work *k1, p1* rib until work measures 3" from CO edge.

Body
Next round: Inc 6 sts evenly across row—80 sts.

Begin chart. Work rounds 1–22 once, then rounds 1–11.

Begin decreasing, switching to dpns when necessary.

K2tog to end of round—40 sts.

Knit 1 round.

K2tog to end of round—20 sts.

Knit 1 round.

K2tog to end of round—10 sts.

Knit 1 round.

K2tog to end of round—5 sts.

Break yarn leaving 12" tail, weave through remaining sts, secure on WS.

Finishing
Weave in all loose ends with tapestry needle. Block lightly.

- ○ yo
- ╱ k2tog
- ☐ knit
- c4 over 4 right
  Sl 4 sts to cn, hold to back, k4, k4 from cn.
- c4 over 4 left
  Sl 4 sts to cn, hold to front, k4, k4 from cn.

SUMMERHOUSE HAT & WRISTERS

Constructed in 1880 and designed by architect Frederick Law Olmsted, the SUMMERHOUSE is a hexagon brick structure that rests on the lawn of the Capitol building. With an oversized Spanish mission tile roof providing plenty of shade, stone benches with seating for 22 people and a water source in the center, it was built to offer shade and rest to those walking the grounds of the Capitol on foot. Filled with interesting stone carvings and wrought iron details, the west side of the structure has a flowing stream referred to as "the Grotto."

A small tree, the OSAGE ORANGE (Maclura pomifera) has both male and female flowers. The bumpy fruit it produces turns yellow in the fall and emits an odor similar to oranges. Elemol, which can be extracted from the fruit, acts as a natural mosquito repellent.

Approximate finished size HAT: One size fits most adults, 20" circumference ✕ WRISTERS: One size fits most adult women, 6½" circumference

Materials HAT: 2 hanks ✕ WRISTERS: 1 hank ✕ Alchemy Yarns of Transformation *Sanctuary* (1¾ oz / 50g; 125 yds / 114m; 30% Silk, 70% Wool) in #65e Dragon ✕ US4 16" circular knitting needle and dpns ✕ Stitch marker, cable needle, tapestry needle

Gauge 23 sts and 32 rows over 4" in stockinette st in the round

Stitch Guide
c3 over 3 right: Sl 3 sts to cn, hold to back, k3, k3 from cn.
c3 over 3 left: Sl 3 sts to cn, hold to front, k3, k3 from cn.

Hat
Brim
CO 116 sts, join into round, being careful not to twist sts, pm for beginning of round.

Work *k1, p1* rib until work measures 1½" from CO edge.

Body
Knit for 1".

K9, yo, ssk, k6, k2tog, yo, knit to end of round.

Knit 1 round.

K8, [yo, ssk] twice, k4, [k2tog, yo] twice, knit to end of round.

Knit 1 round.

K7, [yo, ssk] three times, k2, [k2tog, yo] three times, knit to end of round.

Knit 1 round.

K8, [yo, ssk] three times, [k2tog, yo] three times, knit to end of round.

Knit 3 rounds.

K11, c3 over 3 right, knit to end of round.

Knit 1 round.

K8, [c3 over 3 left] twice, knit to end of round.

Knit 1 round.

K11, c3 over 3 right, knit to end of round.

Knit 3 rounds.

Begin decreases
K7, [k2tog, yo] three times, k2, [yo, ssk] three times, knit to end of round.

Knit 1 round.

K6, [k2tog, yo] three times, k4, [yo, ssk] three times, knit to end of round.

Knit 1 round.

K7, [k2tog, yo] twice, k6, [yo, ssk] twice, knit to end of round.

Knit 1 round.

K8, k2tog, yo, k8, yo, ssk, knit to end of round.

Work in stockinette until work measures 7" from CO edge.

K2tog to end of round—58 sts.

Knit 1 round.

K2tog to end of round—29 sts.

Knit 1 round.

K2tog to last st, k1—15 sts.

Knit 1 round.

K2tog to last st, k1—8 sts.

Break yarn leaving 12" tail, weave through remaining sts, secure on WS. Weave in all loose ends with tapestry needle.

Finishing
Block.

Left Wrister
Cuff
CO 38 sts, divide evenly over dpns join into round, being careful not to twist sts, pm for beginning of round.

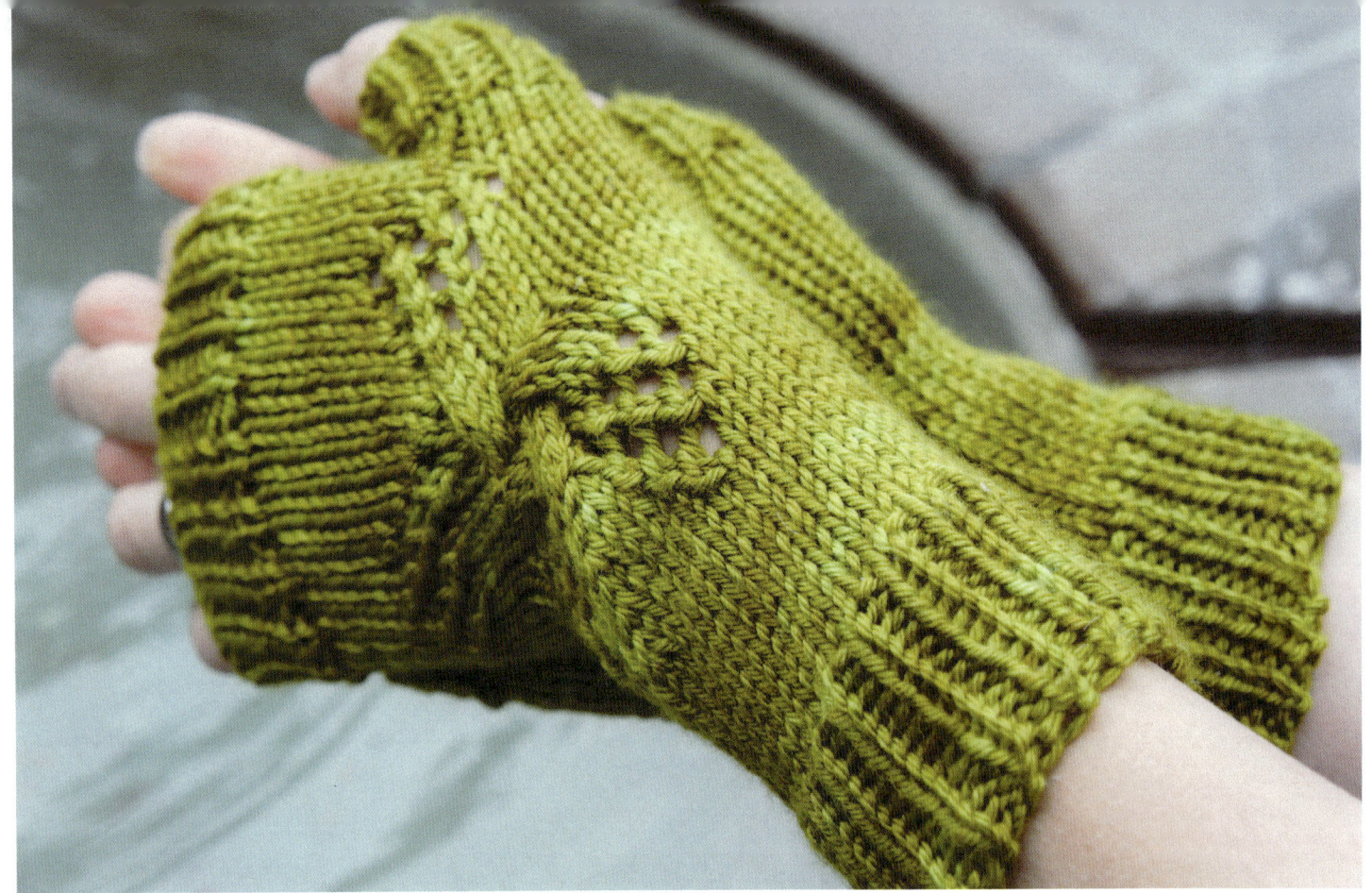

Work *k1, p1* rib until work measures 1½" from CO edge.

Body

Knit for 1".

K9, yo, ssk, k6, k2tog, yo, knit to end of round.

Knit 1 round.

K8, [yo, ssk] twice, k4, [k2tog, yo] twice, knit to end of round.

Knit 1 round.

K7, [yo, ssk] three times, k2, [k2tog, yo] three times, knit to end of round.

Knit 1 round.

K8, [yo, ssk] three times, [k2tog, yo] three times, knit to end of round.

Knit 3 rounds

K11, c3 over 3 right, knit to end of round.

Knit 1 round.

K8, [c3 over 3 left] twice, knit to end of round.

Knit 1 round.

K11, c3 over 3 right, knit to end of round.

Knit 3 rounds.

K6, place these 6 sts on st holder for thumb, k1, [k2tog, yo] three times, k2, [yo, ssk] three times, knit to end of round.

CO 6 sts over gap, knit to end of round.

K6, [k2tog, yo] three times, k4, [yo, ssk] three times, knit to end of round.

Knit 1 round.

K7, [k2tog, yo] twice, k6, [yo, ssk] twice, knit to end of round.

Knit 1 round.

K8, k2tog, yo, k8, yo, ssk, knit to end of round.

Work in stockinette for 1".

Work *k1, p1* for 1".

BO in rib.

Thumb
Remove 6 sts from st holder and put on needles, pick up 1 st from each side, and pick up 6 sts from CO sts, divide evenly over dpns—14 sts.

Knit 5 rounds.

Work *k1, p1* rib for 1".

BO in rib.

Finishing
Weave in all loose ends with tapestry needle. Close gap between hand and thumb.

Block.

Right Wrister
Work as left wrister until first lace row.

K19, yo, ssk, k6, k2tog, yo, knit to end of round.

Knit 1 round.

K18, [yo, ssk] twice, k4, [k2tog, yo] twice, knit to end of round.

Knit 1 round.

K17, [yo, ssk] three times, k2, [k2tog, yo] three times, knit to end of round.

Knit 1 round.

K18, [yo, ssk] three times, [k2tog, yo] three times, knit to end of round.

Knit 3 rounds.

K21, c3 over 3 left, knit to end of round.

Knit 1 round.

K18, [c3 over 3 right] twice, knit to end of round.

Knit 1 round.

K21, c3 over 3 left, knit to end of round.

Knit 3 rounds.

K17, [k2tog, yo] three times, k2, [yo, ssk] three times, knit to last 6 sts, k6, place these 6 sts on st holder for thumb.

Knit to thumb, CO 6 sts over gap.

K16, [k2tog, yo] three times, k4, [yo, ssk] three times, knit to end of round.

Knit 1 round.

K17, [k2tog, yo] twice, k6, [yo, ssk] twice, knit to end of round.

Knit 1 round.

K18, k2tog, yo, k8, yo, ssk, knit to end of round.

Finish as for left wrister.

RENWICK WRISTERS

Approximate finished size One size fits most adults, 7" circumference

Materials Sublime / KFI *Lustrous Extrafine Merino DK* (.88 oz / 25g; approx 104 yds / 95m; 67% Extrafine Merino Wool, 33% Nylon): 1 ball each in #295 Flinty (A) and #293 Saffron (B) ✕ US6 dpns ✕ Stitch marker, cable needle, tapestry needle

Gauge 22 sts and 30 rows over 4" in stockinette st

Completed in 1874 and housing American craft and decorative arts from the 19th to 21st centuries, the museum was named after architect James Renwick, Jr. Originally the Corcoran Gallery of Art, *the building was temporarily used as a military warehouse during the Civil War. The collection quickly outgrew the space and the Corcoran moved down the street into a larger structure in 1897. In 1972 the* Renwick Gallery *became part of the Smithsonian after Jackie Kennedy led the effort to save it and reopened it as a museum for arts and crafts. The paintings are hung salon-style and run 40 feet from floor to ceiling.*

The primary and best source for maple sugar, the Sugar Maple *(Acer saccharum) is easy to spot in the fall due to its bright foliage ranging from yellow to red-orange. One of the most shade-tolerant trees, it is prone to rapid growth in all soil types. Bowling pins and flooring are often made from the wood.*

Stitch Guide
6-st SC
Sl 2 sts to cn and hold to back, k1, k1 from cn, wyib sl 2nd st from cn to right hand needle, sl next st to cn and hold to front, wyib sl next st, k1, k1 from cn.

Left Wrister
With A, CO 34 sts, join into round, being careful not to twist sts, pm for beginning of round.

Begin corrugated ribbing
Setup round: [With A k1, with B p1] to end.

Work previous round until ribbing measures 2½".

Body
Next round: With A, inc 11 sts around—45 sts.
Next round: With A, knit across 22 sts, begin gusset as follows: pm, m1, k1, m1, pm, knit to end.

Begin chart at round 1 over last 22 sts, AT SAME TIME work gusset increase as above every third round.

Work in pattern until there are 15 gusset sts.

Next round: Continue working in pattern, sl gusset sts onto scrap yarn.

Continue in pattern until 8 repeats total are complete.

Switch back to corrugated ribbing and work for 1".

BO in A.

Thumb
Remove 15 sts from waste yarn, pick up 1 st in gap—16 sts.

Work in corrugated ribbing for 1".

BO in A.

Right Wrister

Work as for Left Wrister until after the first 2 rows of body have been worked. Then begin chart at round 1 over the first 22 sts (Left Wrister was worked over the last 22 sts).

Work rest of directions as for Left Wrister.

Finishing

Weave in all loose ends with tapestry needle, close gap between hand and thumb.

Block lightly.

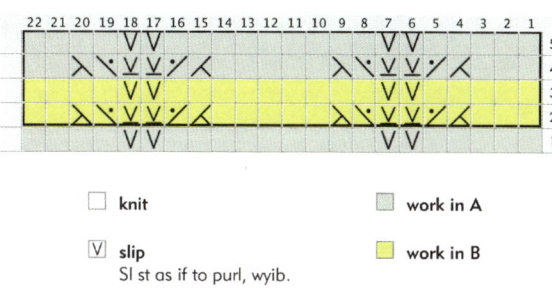

☐ knit

☑ slip
Sl st as if to purl, wyib.

⧖ 6-st SC
Sl 2 sts to cn and hold to back, k1, k1 from cn, wyib sl 2nd st from cn to right needle, sl next st to cn and hold to front, wyib sl next st, k1, k1 from cn.

▨ work in A

▨ work in B

CONSTITUTION HALL SCARF

Approximate finished size 10" wide by 70" long

Materials Viola *Silky DK* (3½ oz / 100g; approx 231 yds / 211m; 50% Superwash Merino, 50% Silk): 2 hanks in Mushroom (A) and 1 hank in Bruised Plum (B) × US6 knitting needles × Waste yarn, tapestry needle

Gauge 17 sts and 38 rows over 4" in garter st

Built in 1929 and designed by John Russell Pope, the Daughters of the American Revolution built the CONSTITUTION HALL *when they outgrew the Memorial Continental Hall. The DAR Library and Museum were later built to connect the two buildings. The largest auditorium in Washington, the hall seats 3,702 people and includes a Presidential box and large pipe organ. Designed in the Neoclassical style, it has an Alabama limestone exterior and an unusual U-shaped balcony. The Hall is used for concerts, commencements, conferences, corporate meetings, televised events and other performances.*

A fast growing small tree, the SWAMP WHITE OAK *(Quercus bicolor) can survive in many conditions and can live to be 350 years old. Easy to transplant, this has become a recent favorite for lumber and landscapers.*

Stitch Guide
m5 sts in one
(K1, yo, k1, yo, k1) in 1 st.

Lace Edging Pattern
Rows 1, 3, 5 (RS): K1b, *[p1, k1b] 2 times, p1, [k1b, p1] 2 times, k1b; repeat from *, end p1.
Rows 2, 4, 6: K1, *p1, k1; repeat from *, end p1.
Row 7: K1b, *[p1, k1b] 2 times, m5 sts in one, [k1b, p1] 2 times, k1b; repeat from *, end p1.
Row 8: K1, *[p1, k1] 2 times, p6, [p1, k1] 2 times; repeat from *, end p1.
Row 9: K1b, *p1, k1b, p1, k2tog, k3, ssk, [p1, k1b] 2 times; repeat from *, end p1.
Row 10: K1, *[p1, k1] 2 times, p5, k1, p1, k1; repeat from *, end p1.
Row 11: K1b, *p1, k1b, k2tog, k3, ssk, k1b, p1, k1b; repeat from *, end p1.
Row 12: K1, *p1, k1, p7, k1; repeat from *, end p1.
Row 13: K1b, *p1, k2tog, yo, k3, yo, ssk, p1, k1b; repeat from *, end p1.
Row 14: K1, *p1, k1, p7, k1; repeat from *, end p1.
Row 15: K1b, *[k2tog, yo]2 times, k1, [yo, k2tog] 2 times, k1b; repeat from *, end p1.
Row 16: P1, *p10; repeat from *, end p1.
Row 17: K2tog, *k3, yo, k1, yo, k3, sk2p; repeat from *.
Row 18: Purl.

Scarf
With A, CO 150 sts.

Knit 4 rows with A (2 garter ridges).

Carrying yarn up along the side, change to B and knit 4 rows.

Work 4 rows alternating A and B until work measures 7" (or for 18 stripes), ending with 4 rows of B.

Do not BO, put sts on waste yarn.

With RS facing, pick up and knit 30 sts along right side of work with B.

Next row (WS): Knit 1 row in B.

Work 2 rows (1 ridge) in A.

Work 2 rows (1 ridge) in B.

Repeat last 2 rows until work measures 35" from pick up and knit.

Work 1 row in A, BO loosely.

Lace Edging

With RS facing, transfer sts from waste yarn to needles and pick up sts across second half with A—302 sts.

Work rows 1–18 of chart with A.

BO loosely.

Finishing

Weave in all loose ends with tapestry needle.

Block well.

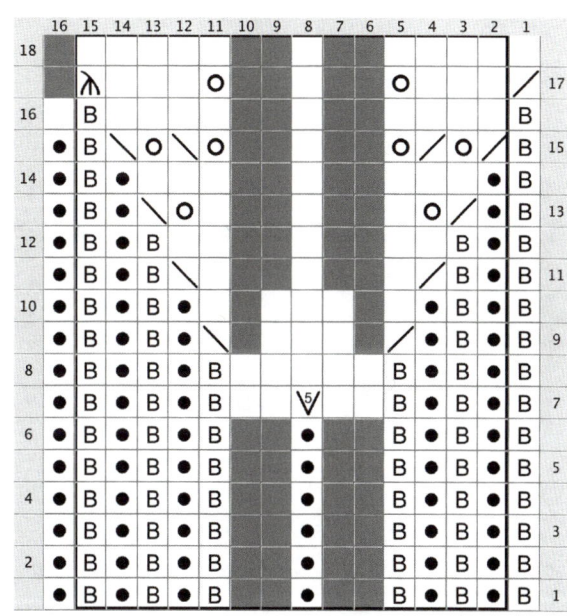

- **B** k1b — RS: k1b, WS: purl
- **•** purl — RS: purl, WS: knit
- ■ no stitch — placeholder—no stitch made
- □ knit — RS: knit, WS: purl
- **V5** m5 sts in one — (K1, yo, k1, yo, k1) in 1 st.
- ╱ k2tog
- ╲ ssk
- **o** yo
- λ sk2p

CAPITOL SHAWL

Approximate finished size 58" wide by 24" deep

Materials 1 hank SweetGeorgia Yarns *Merino Silk DK* (3½ oz / 100g; 380 yds / 347m; 50% Fine Merino Wool, 50% Cultivated Silk) in Pistachio (A) ✕ 18 yds Colinette Yarns *Cadenza* (per hank: 1¾ oz / 50g; approx 132 yds / 121m; 100% Merino) in Vincent's Apron (B) ✕ 1 ball Sirdar *Baby Bamboo* (1¾ oz / 50g; approx 105 yds / 96m; 80% Bamboo, 20% Wool) in #132 Putty (C) ✕ US9 knitting needles ✕ Stitch markers, tapestry needle

Gauge 12½ sts and 19 rows over 4" in stockinette st, blocked

Housing the meeting chambers of both the Senate and the House, the Capitol building *is also the location for presidential inaugurations, lying in state and contains many historical artifacts. Built in marble-covered brick with a cast iron dome that weighs over 8,909,200 pounds and capped with the Statue of Freedom, the site was found by George Washington with plans originally drawn by William Thornton. The main building was completed in 1826, but with new construction as recent as 2008, the building continues to grow and improve.*

A member of the magnolia family, the American Tulip *(Liriodendron tulipifera) has large flowers that resemble tulips. A fine-grained and stable wood, it is often used for cabinets and furniture. Often called "canoewood," the trees were used for dugout canoes by Eastern Native Americans.*

Body

With A, CO 2 sts, knit 10 rows (garter st), turn work horizontal, pick up and knit 5 sts in garter edge sts, turn work and pick up and knit 2 original CO sts—9 sts.

Row 1 (WS): K2, pm, p2, pm, p1, pm, p2, pm, k2.

Row 2 (RS): K2, slm, yo, knit to marker, slm, yo, knit to marker, yo, slm, knit to marker, yo, slm, k2—4 sts inc.

Row 3: K2, slipping all markers purl across to last 2 sts, k2.

Repeat rows 2 and 3 14 times (28 rows)—65 sts.

Switch to B, work rows 2 and 3.

Switch to A, work rows 2 and 3.

Continue in this manner until there are 6 stripes in B—109 sts.

Switch to A and work rows 2 and 3 11 more times (22 rows)—153 sts.

Next row: Switch to C, k2, slm, yo, k39, slm, yo, k35, pm, yo, k1, yo, pm, k35, yo, slm, k39, yo, slm, k2—159 sts.

Next row: K2, slipping all markers purl across to last 2 sts, k2.

Next row: K2, slm, yo, knit to marker, slm, yo, knit to marker, slm, yo, knit to marker, yo, slm, knit to marker, yo, slm, knit to marker, yo, slm, k2—6 sts inc.

Switch to A, work last 2 rows.

Switch to C, work last 2 rows.

Continue in this manner until there are 9 stripes in C—255 sts.

Edging

Rows 1, 3 and 7 (RS): Switch to A, knit, inc 1 st across—256 sts.
Rows 2 and 4 (WS): Purl.
Row 5: *K2tog, [yo] twice, ssk, repeat to end of row.
Row 6: *P1, (k1, p1, k1, p1, k1) in double yo, p1, repeat to end of row.
Row 8: BO knitwise.

Finishing

Block well.

NATIONAL GALLERY SHAWL

Approximate finished size 50" wide by 16" long

Materials 2-COLOR VERSION: 1 hank Knit Collage *Stargazer Silk & Sequins* (3½ oz / 100g; approx 100 yds / 91m; 100% Silk with bass sequins) in Blue Lagoon (A) and 2 balls Sublime / KFI *Lustrous Extrafine Merino DK* (.88 oz / 25g; approx 104yds / 95m; 67% Extrafine Merino Wool, 33% Nylon) in 298 Sealskin (B) ✕ 1-COLOR VERSION: 2 hanks Sanguine Gryphon *Codex* (4 oz / 113g; approx 234 yds / 214m; 52% Silk, 48% Blue-faced Leicester Wool) in The Vulgar Bootman ✕ US 9 knitting needles and dpns ✕ 4 stitch markers, tapestry needle

Gauge 12½ sts and 25 rows over 4" in stockinette st, blocked

The NATIONAL GALLERY OF ART *consists of two main buildings connected by an underground passage covered in 41,000 LEDs running the entire length. The West building was built in 1941 and designed by architect John Russell Pope in the Neoclassical style using pink Tennessee marble. It houses works from the European masters from the medieval period through the 19th century. The geometrical East building designed by I.M. Pei in 1978 sits in stark contrast and houses modern and contemporary art with an open atrium and bell tower. The outdoor Sculpture Garden was completed in 1999 and is home to large sculpture, a pond and fountain.*

Called the WHITE OAK *(Quercus alba), this tree actually has a gray bark and an edible acorn. Often growing as wide as it is tall, this hardwood can live to be 600 years old. A strong, heavy, fine-grained wood, it is water and rot-resistant, making it perfect for whiskey and wine barrels, martial arts weapons and construction.*

Stitch Guide
cluster
Wyif slip 5, dropping extra 2 wraps, [bring yarn to back between needles, slip 5 sts to left needle, bring yarn to front between needles, slip 5 sts to right] twice.

Daisy Chain Pattern
Row 1 (RS): Knit.
Row 2 (WS): Knit.
Row 3: K1, *[k1 wrapping yarn 3 times around needle] 5 times, k1* repeat from * to end of row.
Row 4: *K1, cluster* repeat from * to last st, k1.
Row 5: Knit.
Row 6: Knit

Lace Edging Pattern
Row 1 (RS): Sl wyif, yo, k2tog, yo, k2tog, k8.
Row 2 (WS): Yo, p3, yo, k2tog, p4, yo, k2tog, p1, join.
Row 3: Sl wyif, yo, k2tog, yo, k2tog, k9.
Row 4: Yo, p5, yo, k2tog, p3, yo, k2tog, p1, join.
Row 5: Sl wyif, yo, k2tog, yo, k2tog, k10.
Row 6: Yo, p1, k2tog, yo, p1, yo, p1, k2tog, yo, k2tog, p2, yo, k2tog, p1, join.
Row 7: Sl wyif, yo, k2tog, yo, k2tog, k11.
Row 8: Yo, p1, k2tog, yo, p3, yo, k2tog, p1, yo, k2tog, p1, yo, k2tog, p1, join.
Row 9: Sl wyif, yo, k2tog, yo, k2tog, k12.
Row 10: Yo, sk2p, p1, yo, sk2p, yo, p1, k2tog, yo, p3, yo, k2tog, p1, join.
Row 11: Sl wyif, yo, k2tog, yo, k2tog, k11.
Row 12: Yo, sk2p, p1, [k2tog] twice, yo, p4, yo, k2tog, p1, join.
Row 13: Sl wyif, yo, k2tog, yo, k2tog, k9.
Row 14: Yo, sk2p, k2tog, yo, p5, yo, k2tog, p1, join.

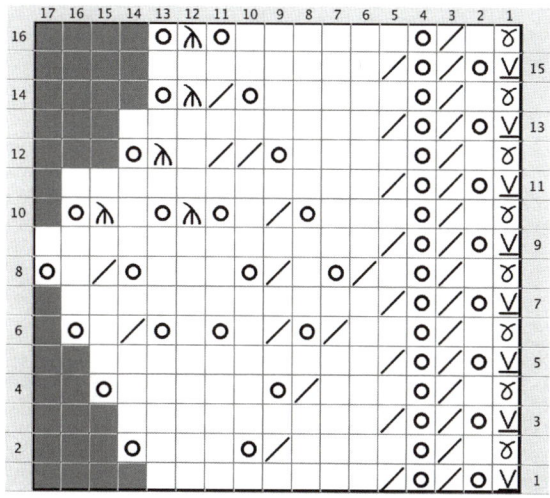

if RS and WS are not specified, definition applies to both sides

- ○ yo
- ╱ k2tog
- ☐ knit
  RS: knit stitch
  WS: purl stitch
- ⋏ sk2p
- V sl wyif
  RS: Sl st as if to purl, wyif.
- 8 join
  WS: Knit border st tbl together with shawl body st.
- ■ no stitch
  placeholder—no stitch made

Row 15: Sl wyif, yo, k2tog, yo, k2tog, k8.
Row 16: Yo, sk2p, yo, p6, yo, k2tog, p1, join.

Body

NOTE: For 2-Color Version, use yarns as directed. below. For 1-Color Version, work entire piece in 1 yarn.

CO 2 sts in A, work 10 rows in garter st, turn work and pick up and knit 5 sts along edge, turn again and pick up and knit 2 original CO sts—9 sts.

Set up row (WS): K2, pm, p2, pm, p1, pm, p2, pm, k2.
Next row (RS): K2, slm, yo, knit to next marker, slm, yo, knit to next marker, yo, slm, knit to last 2 sts, yo, slm, k2—4 sts inc.
Next row: K2, purl to last 2 sts, k2.

Work the previous 2 rows until there are 73 sts on needle.

Switch to B and work rows 1–6 of Daisy Chain Pattern.

Switch to A and work until there are 85 sts on needle.

Switch to B and work rows 1–6 of Daisy Chain Pattern.

Switch to A and work until there 97 sts on needle.

Switch to B and work rows 1–6 of Daisy Chain Pattern.

Switch to A and work until there are 121 sts on needle, ending on RS row.

Next row (WS): K2, purl to last 2 sts, k2tog—120 sts.

Do not BO, leave sts on needle.

Lace Edging

With RS facing and using B, starting at bottom right edge, CO 13 sts on one dpn.

Begin chart, join on all WS rows.

Work a total of 15 reps.

BO loosely knitwise.

Finishing

Weave in all loose ends with tapestry needle.

Block well.

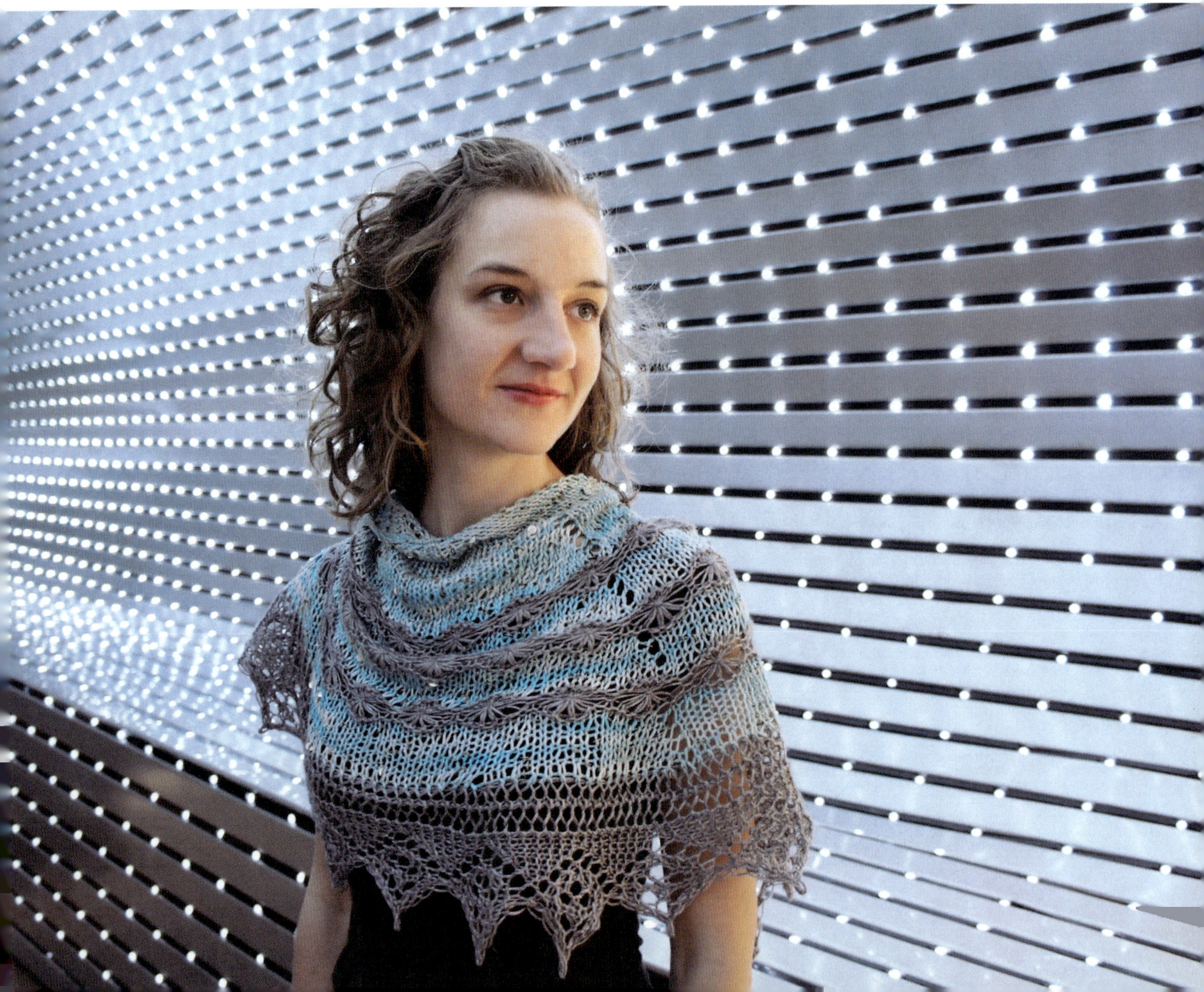

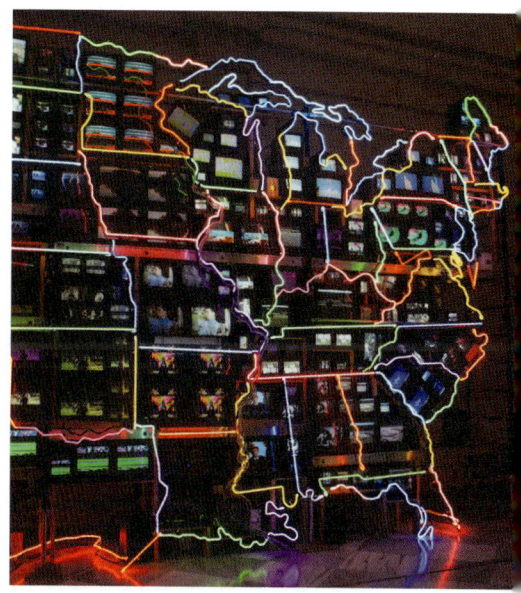

ABBREVIATIONS

6-st SC: Slip 2 stitches to cable needle and hold to back, knit 1, knit 1 from cable needle, with yarn in back slip second stitch from cable needle to right hand needle, slip next stitch to cable needle and hold to front, with yarn in back slip next stitch, knit 1, knit 1 from cable needle.

approx: approximately

BO: Bind Off

c3 over 3 right: Slip 3 stitches to cable needle, hold to back, knit 3, knit 3 from cable needle.

c3 over 3 left: Slip 3 stitches to cable needle, hold to front, knit 3, knit 3 from cable needle.

c4 over 4 right: Slip 4 stitches to cable needle, hold to back, knit 4, knit 4 from cable needle.

c4 over 4 left: Slip 4 stitches to cable needle, hold to front, knit 4, knit 4 from cable needle.

cluster: With yarn in front slip 5 stitches, dropping extra 2 wraps, [bring yarn to back between needles, slip 5 stitches to left hand needle, bring yarn to front between needles, slip 5 stitches to right hand needle] twice.

cn: cable needle

CO: Cast On

dec: decrease(d)

dpn(s): double pointed needle(s)

inc: increase(d)

k: knit

k1b: knit 1 stitch through the back loop

k2tog: knit 2 stitches together

k2togb: knit 2 stitches together through the back loops

m1: make one

m5 sts in one: (knit 1, yarn over, knit 1, yarn over, knit 1) in one stitch

p: purl

p2tog: purl 2 stitches together

p2togb: Insert needle from the left, behind and into the backs of the 2nd and 1st stitches in that order. Purl 2 stitches together.

pm: place marker

rep(s): repeat(s)

RS: Right Side

sk2p: slip 1 stitch, knit 2 together, pass slipped stitch over

sl: slip

slm: slip marker

ssk: Slip 1 stitch as if to knit, slip another stitch as if to knit. Insert left hand needle into fronts of these 2 stitches and knit together.

st(s): stitch(es)

WS: Wrong Side

wyib: with yarn in back

wyif: with yarn in front

yo: yarn over

Pattern Skill Levels

Beginner ☆　Intermediate ☆☆　Advanced ☆☆☆

Knitting Needle Conversion

Metric (mm)	US	UK / Canada
2.0	0	14
2.25	1	13
2.75	2	12
3.0	-	11
3.25	3	10
3.5	4	-
3.75	5	9
4.0	6	8
4.5	7	7
5.0	8	6
5.5	9	5
6.0	10	4
6.5	10½	3
7.0	-	2
7.5	-	1
8.0	11	0
9.0	13	00
10.0	15	000
12.0	17	-
16.0	19	-
19.0	35	-
25.0	50	-

Crochet Hook Conversion

Metric (mm)	US	UK / Canada
4.0	G / 6	8
6.0	J / 10	4

Length Conversion

1.09 yds = 1m   109 yds = 100m

Yards to meters: # of yards x 0.914
Meters to yards: # of meters x 1.09

Weight Conversion

1¾ oz = 50g   3½ oz = 100g

Ounces to grams: # of ounces x 28.35
Grams to ounces: # of grams x 0.035

RESOURCES

1. **Alchemy Yarns of Transformation**
   PO Box 1080
   Sebastopol, CA 95473
   707.823.3276
   www.alchemyyarns.com

2. **Artyarns**
   39 Westmoreland Avenue
   White Plains, NY 10606
   914.428.0333
   www.artyarns.com

3. **Blue Sky Alpacas**
   PO Box 88
   Cedar, MN 55011
   763.753.5815
   www.blueskyalpacas.com

4. **Brooklyn Tweed**
   www.brooklyntweed.net

5. **Colinette**
   Banwy Workshops
   Llanfair Caereinion
   Powys, SY210SG
   UK
   01938.810128
   www.colinette.com

6. **Imperial Yarn**
   92462 Hinton Road
   Maupin, OR 97037
   541.395.2507
   www.imperialyarn.com

7. **Knit Collage**
   Boston, MA
   610.999.5063
   www.knitcollage.com

8. **Madelinetosh**
   7515 Benbrook Parkway
   Benbrook, TX 76126
   817.249.3066
   www.madelinetosh.com

9. **Red Barn Yarn**
   450 Rosemont Avenue
   Pasadena, CA 91103
   626.221.8817
   www.redbarnyarn.com

10. **Sanguine Gryphon**
    www.sanguinegryphon.com

11 **Sirdar**
Distributed by KFI
PO Box 336-315
Bayview Avenue
Amityville, NY 11701
516.546.3600
www.knittingfever.com

12 **Sublime**
Distributed by KFI
PO Box 336-315
Bayview Avenue
Amityville, NY 11701
516.546.3600
www.knittingfever.com

13 **SweetGeorgia Yarns**
401-228 East 4th Avenue, buzz 164
Vancouver, BC
V5T 1G5
Canada
604.569.6811
www.sweetgeorgiayarns.com

14 **Viola**
www.etsy.com/shop/violaviola

Design, Knitting & Photography
Tanis Gray

Technical Editing
Amy Polcyn

Model
Jess Dekker

Illustration
Paul Heaston

Graphic Design
Mary Joy Gumayagay

Special Thanks
Roger Chang
Mary Joy Gumayagay
Autumn Parker
Becky Deux

Made in the USA
Charleston, SC
18 October 2012